W9-BYX-907

I See Red

Trudy Micco

Bailey Books
an imprint of
Enslow Publishers, Inc.
40 Industrial Road
Box 398
Berkeley Heights, NJ 07922
USA
http://www.enslow.com

Bailey Books, an imprint of Enslow Publishers, Inc.

Library of Congress Cataloging-in-Publication Data

Micco, Trudy.
I see red / Trudy Micco.
p. cm. — (All about colors)
Summary: "Learn about the color red"— Provided by publisher.
  Includes bibliographical references and index.
ISBN 978-0-7660-3787-8
1. Red—Juvenile literature. 2. Color—Juvenile literature. I. Title.
QC495.5.M477 2011
535.6—dc22

                                    2010011874

Paperback ISBN: 978-1-59845-162-7

Printed in the United States of America

062010 Lake Book Manufacturing, Inc., Melrose Park, IL

10 9 8 7 6 5 4 3 2 1

To Our Readers: We have done our best to make sure all Internet Addresses in this book
were active and appropriate when we went to press. However, the author and the publisher
have no control over and assume no liability for the material available on those Internet sites
or on other Web sites they may link to. Any comments or suggestions can be sent by e-mail
to comments@enslow.com or to the address on the back cover.

♻ Enslow Publishers, Inc., is committed to printing our books on recycled paper. The paper
in every book contains 10% to 30% post-consumer waste (PCW). The cover board on the
outside of each book contains 100% PCW. Our goal is to do our part to help young people
and the environment too!

Photo Credits: Shutterstock.com

Cover Photo: Shutterstock.com

Note to Parents and Teachers

Help pre-readers get a jumpstart on reading. These lively stories introduce simple concepts
with repetition of words and short simple sentences. Photos and illustrations fill the pages
with color and effectively enhance the text. Free Educator Guides are available for this series
at www.enslow.com. Search for the *All About Colors* series name.

Contents

Words to Know

red

hat

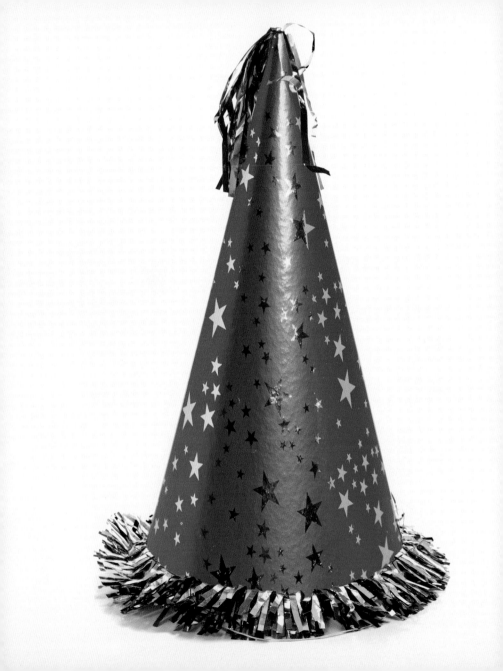

Where is my red hat?

It is not here.

Where is my red hat?

It is not here.

Where is my red hat?

It is not here.

Where is my red hat?

It is not here.

Where is my red hat?

It is on my head!

Read More

Bruce, Lisa. *Red.* Chicago, Ill.: Raintree, 2004.

Sidman, Joyce. *Red Sings From Treetops: A Year in Colors.* Boston: Houghton Mifflin Books for Children, 2009.

Web Sites

Chateau MeddyBemps *A Rainbow of Frogs.* <http://www.meddybemps.com/9.500.html>

Do2Learn. *What Color?* <http://www.do2learn.com/games/whatcolor/pages/index.html>

Index

Guided Reading Level: **B**
Guided Reading Leveling System is based on the guidelines recommended by Fountas and Pinnell.

Word Count: 46